Play Animal Game!

by Anne Schreiber and Gail Tuchman
Illustrated by Tim Haggerty

SCHOLASTIC

All animals are not the same.

Read these hints,

Then call out the name

Of each animal in this game.

This animal eats seeds

And acts like a duck.

It does not quack.

It says, "cluck, cluck."

Can you name it?

It's a hen.

This animal is black

And so very small.

If you blink,

You can't see it at all.

It's an ant.

This little animal

Can smell as bad as can be.

If it blocks your path,

Then don't blame me!

It's a skunk.

This animal swims in the sea.

It has a funny smell.

It blends in with the plants

And lives in a clean shell.

It's a clam.

This animal can rise like a plane.

On cliffs and trees it nests.

It can flap and flap and flap,

Then find a place to rest.

It's a bird.

This small animal is very wet.

It lives in a clean pond.

It eats up many, many bugs.

On blades of grass it hops.

It's a frog.

Now that you see

All animals are not the same,

Make up some other hints,

And play the animal game!

My Words

*animal
*find
*funny
*small

bl-	cl-	pl-
black	clam	place
blades	clean	plane
blame	cliffs	plants
blends	cluck	play
blink		
blocks		

*new high frequency words

ISBN: 0-590-99862-5   Copyright © 1997 by Scholastic Inc.   All rights reserved.   Printed in the U.S.A.